Focus on the SEASONS

Focus on
SUMMER

By Rosie Seaman

Fearon Teacher Aids
Simon & Schuster Supplementary Education Group

ABOUT THE AUTHOR

Rosie Seaman is an educator, author, and television producer. She has written several books for children and her work has been highlighted in a number of national magazines. As director of children's programming for WKRG-TV in Mobile, Alabama, Ms. Seaman has developed a variety of educational programs for young children.

Ms. Seaman received her certification in the Montessori method of preschool education and bases her work on the Montessori philosophy that young children learn best through techniques that encourage manipulation, experimentation, and discovery of the world around them.

Editorial Director: Virginia L. Murphy

Editors: Marilyn Trow and Sue Mogard

Copyeditor: Lisa Schwimmer

Design: Terry McGrath

Production: Rebecca Speakes

Cover Design: Lucyna Green

Cover and Inside Illustration: Marilynn Barr

ISBN 0-86653-972-7

Contents

A Note from the Author

The *Focus on the Seasons* series teaches basic skills, concepts, and subject matter to young children through active participation and discovery. Arranged in four seasonal books, the activities offer young learners the opportunity to express themselves freely throughout the school year as they contribute to their school environment.

Focus on Summer helps children discover some of the changes of this exciting season. Children learn about plants, insects, and animals, participate in physical activities that promote the use of large motor skills, enjoy summer through art, and celebrate summer holidays with their families.

Invite the children to help set up an area in the classroom for sharing completed projects about summer. For example, a specific wall space and table may be used to display the children's creations. Displaying children's work is important to reinforce visually the skills and concepts they learn each day.

Use this book as a way of opening many other exciting avenues for exploring summer with the children. The results will be an accumulation of endless treasures that will always be of great value to both you and your young students. Have fun together!

Rosie Seaman

Introduction

The *Focus on the Seasons* series encourages you, the teacher, to be actively involved with the children and their learning. Each seasonal book provides children with an opportunity to learn about the seasons, as well as one another, through hands-on experiences with a variety of materials.

The format of each book offers easy reference to activities that explore commonly used early-childhood units, as well as suggesting a hands-on approach for implementing the activities into existing programs. Each book presents simple directions and bold illustrations and includes a bibliography of quality children's books to enhance the seasonal themes.

The activities begin with a list of materials to gather and offer suggested discussion questions. Each activity provides a step-by-step process for involving the children and suggests other alternatives when appropriate.

A SUGGESTED APPROACH

Prior to each activity:

➤ invite the children into the activity with the discussion questions, expanding the ideas presented in the questions as the children show interest.

➤ display the suggested materials on a low table in a work area that encourages the children to work independently.

During each activity:

➤ encourage the children to express their unique ideas through the materials.

➤ become involved with the children through conversations or mutual participation in the projects.

Following each activity:

➤ place the materials in a learning center in the classroom for the children to explore during independent time.

➤ display the children's completed creations in the classroom for you and the children to enjoy.

OBSERVING THE CHANGES OF SUMMER

SUMMER is a season filled with many changes. Through hands-on activities, the children will discover the signs of summer, the properties of water and some summer fun that water provides, and make fun, summer snacks to enjoy.

Fun in the Sun

MATERIALS

➤ crayons
➤ white construction paper
➤ thinned, yellow tempera paint
➤ paintbrushes

SHARING TOGETHER

➤ What do you like best about summer? What do you like to do in the warm summer sun? How do you keep cool on hot summer days?

➤ Have you ever been to a beach? What did you do there? Have you ever been to a swimming pool? What else do you like to do in the summer? Do you like to go for walks? Do you go to the zoo? What do you see at the zoo?

WORKING TOGETHER

Invite the children to draw pictures of their favorite summer activities, such as swimming at the beach or pool, playing outside with friends, or taking a walk with the family. Give each child a sheet of white construction paper and crayons. Encourage the children to be creative as they draw. After they have completed their pictures, brush thinned, yellow tempera paint over the drawings to represent sunshine. Display the pictures on a bulletin board labeled "Fun in the Sun!"

Sun Sandwiches

MATERIALS

- bread slices
- pimento cheese (or another yellow or orange sandwich spread)
- olives, pickles, and pimento pieces
- square cheese slices
- large, round cookie cutters
- butter knives
- paper plates

PIMENTO CHEESE SPREAD

SHARING TOGETHER

➤ What do you think is the sun's job? What does the sun give us? Does the sun give us heat? Does the sun give us light? Did you know that plants, animals, and people all need the sun to grow? What other things help us grow (water, food, and so on)?

WORKING TOGETHER

Invite the children to join you in making sun sandwiches. Ask the children to wash their hands and then help you clean off a work table surface. Help the children use cookie cutters to cut circles from the bread slices. Place the bread slices on paper plates. Using butter knives, show the children how to spread cheese on the bread circles to make suns. Invite the children to use pimento pieces, olives, and pickles to create facial features. Then cut square cheese slices into four triangles. Encourage the children to arrange the cheese triangles around the bread circles to make rays of sunlight. Invite the children to enjoy eating their sunny summertime snacks!

Summer Shapes

MATERIALS

➤ crayons

➤ white construction paper

➤ geometric shapes cut from colored construction paper

➤ glue

SHARING TOGETHER

➤ What do you see outside that is round? (Show the children something outside that is round.) Is a tree round? How about the sun? What do you see in the room that is round? Can you show me?

➤ Let's look outside. Can you find something outside that is square? (Show the children something outside that is square.) Is a flower square? How about a house? Some houses are square, aren't they? What other things can you think of that are square? Can you find something that is square in the classroom?

WORKING TOGETHER

Place the materials listed on page 12 on a work table within easy reach of the children. Give each child a sheet of white construction paper. Invite the children to arrange and glue a variety of geometric shapes on the construction paper to make summer pictures or designs. Encourage the children to use their imaginations. Suggest to the children that they use crayons to add details to their pictures. Or, children can make pictures from just one of the shapes, such as a sun or an apple from a circle, a gift or a window from a square, and so on. Display the pictures on a Sharing Wall in the classroom.

A Beach Bag

MATERIALS

➤ white pillowcases (one per child)

➤ liquid embroidery pens (may be purchased at a hobby or art shop)

➤ pencils

SHARING TOGETHER

➤ Do you like to go to the beach? What would you take with you if you went to the beach? Would you take a snow shovel? How about a winter coat? How about a towel? Name some other things you might take if you were to go to the beach.

➤ What do you like to do at the beach? Do you know how to swim? Have you ever made a sand castle? What else can you do at the beach?

WORKING TOGETHER

Invite the children to make summer beach bags. Give each child a pillowcase (or send a note home asking parents to give their child an old pillowcase to bring to school). Place the pillowcases flat on a work table. Invite the children to use liquid embroidery pens to draw summer objects on their pillowcases, such as a beach ball, shell, sun, and so on. Children may want to draw their pictures or designs with pencil first. Then, when they have made the design they want, the children can trace over the pencil drawings with their embroidery pens. After the ink dries thoroughly, encourage the children to use their beach bags for summer outings!

Float or Sink

MATERIALS

➤ large, clear container of water

➤ small items from the classroom that can be immersed in water, such as plastic blocks, cups, fruit, soap, paper clips, and so on

➤ towels

➤ large sheet of tagboard

SHARING TOGETHER

➤ Do you like to go swimming in the summer? Where do you go swimming? Do you know how to float on the water? Let's pretend we are in the water and we are floating.

➤ Show the children two small items from the classroom that can be immersed in water. Here is a (plastic cup) and here is a (paper clip). Which one do you think will sink? Which one do you think will float? Let's place these items in the water. Did you guess correctly?

WORKING TOGETHER

Divide a sheet of tagboard into two columns and print "Sink" across the top of one column and "Float" across the top of the other. Place the materials within easy reach of the children on a work table and invite the children to gather around. Encourage the children to take turns placing the items in the water. Make sure the items are small enough to immerse in the water container, as well as small enough to place on the tagboard. Ask the children to predict whether each item will sink or float. Then show the children how to dry each item with a towel and then place the items on the appropriate columns on the tagboard.

A Soap Sailboat

MATERIALS

➤ flat bars of soap, one for each child (Ivory works best)

➤ wooden stir sticks

➤ scissors

➤ construction paper

➤ paper punch

➤ a large container of water

SHARING TOGETHER

➤ Have you ever been on a boat? What kind of boat? Tell us about it. Do you know why boats have sails? Why? How does the wind help a sailboat move? What else helps boats move (oars, motors)?

➤ Do you think soap will float or sink in water? Let's see. Did you guess correctly?

WORKING TOGETHER

Invite the children to make sailboats out of soap. Give each child a small bar of soap. Ask the children to insert a wooden stir stick in the center of the soap with help from an adult or older student. Then show the children how to make sails for their soap boats. Help the children cut construction-paper triangles for the sails. Punch a hole in two corners of the triangles, then slide the triangles over the wooden stir sticks, making sure the stir sticks go through both holes. Invite the children to sail their soap sailboats in a large container of water.

Life Preservers

MATERIALS

➤ a life preserver (or a picture of one)

➤ doughnuts

➤ jam

➤ chopped nuts

➤ string licorice

➤ butter knives

GRAPE JAM

SHARING TOGETHER

➤ Do you know what a life preserver is? (Show the children a life preserver or a picture of a life preserver.) When might you use a life preserver? Did you know that a life preserver helps you stay safe in the water? (Explain the use of a life preserver to the children. Discuss important water safety rules, too. For example, explain to the children that they should never go swimming without an adult.)

WORKING TOGETHER

Invite the children to make life preservers they can eat! Ask the children to wash their hands and then help you clean off a work table surface. Slice the doughnuts in half lengthwise and give each child two halves. Invite the children to spread jam on each doughnut half and sprinkle nuts on top of the jam. Be aware that some children may have allergies to nuts. Check with the children's parents beforehand. Then have the children put their doughnut halves back together. Show the children how to wrap licorice strings around the doughnuts to represent rope and then join the children in eating the life-preserver treats.

Let's Make Lemonade!

MATERIALS

➤ card table

➤ butcher paper

➤ marking pens or crayons

➤ lemons, sugar, water, and ice (or use packaged lemonade mix)

➤ plastic pitchers or containers

➤ large mixing spoons

➤ knife (for adult use only)

➤ paper cups

➤ masking tape

LEMONADE FOR SALE

SHARING TOGETHER

➤ Where do lemons come from? Did you know that lemons grow on trees? Have you ever eaten a lemon? Was it sweet, like an orange? Let's taste a lemon. (Cut a lemon into small pieces for the children to taste.) Does it taste sweet or sour?

➤ Do you like lemonade? Do you know how to make lemonade? What do you need to make lemonade (lemon juice, sugar, and water)? Have you ever sold lemonade at a lemonade stand? Tell us about it.

WORKING TOGETHER

Explain to the children that they will be helping you make lemonade for a lemonade stand and that on a designated day, you and the children will invite family members and other classes to come and buy some lemonade from you at school. Discuss with the children the price of each glass of lemonade, as well as what the money collected will be used for. Include the children in on deciding what you will do with the money, such as using it for a special field trip or a class party. You may want to suggest using the money for a good cause as well.

Divide the class into two groups. On a large piece of butcher paper, write in large letters, "Lemonade for Sale," or some other eye-catching phrase. Then place the butcher paper on the floor. Ask one group of children to decorate the sign with marking pens or crayons. Then ask the other group of children to wash their hands and help you make fresh lemonade (use a packaged lemonade mix or make lemonade from scratch).

On the designated day, place a card table in an open area of the classroom or set up the lemonade stand outside. Invite the guests to buy and sample your summertime drink. Encourage the children to help pour, take money, and so on.

A Nutshell Boat

MATERIALS

➤ walnut shell halves

➤ toothpicks

➤ foil

➤ clay

➤ glue

➤ scissors

➤ a large container of water

ALUMINUM FOIL

SHARING TOGETHER

➤ Have you ever been on a boat? Tell us about your boat trip. What kind of boat were you on?

➤ Can you name some different kinds of boats (fishing boat, motorboat, sailboat, and so on)? Do you know how boats move in the water? How does a sailboat move through the water? Have you ever been in a canoe? How does a canoe move?

WORKING TOGETHER

Explain to the children that they will be making their own small boats from a nutshell. Give each child a walnut shell half and a small piece of clay. Invite the children to roll the clay into small balls and place them inside their walnut shell halves. Help the children cut triangles from tin foil and then glue the triangles on toothpicks to make sails. When the glue has dried completely, encourage the children to stick the toothpick sails into the clay in the walnut shell halves. Invite the children to float their sailboats in a large container of water. Suggest that they blow on the sails to make the sailboats move.

A Sailboat Salad

MATERIALS

- ➤ a life jacket (or a picture of one)
- ➤ peach halves
- ➤ lettuce leaves
- ➤ pretzel sticks
- ➤ square cheese slices (cut in triangular shapes)
- ➤ paper plates

PEACH HALVES

SHARING TOGETHER

➤ Do you know how to stay safe in a boat? Have you ever worn a life jacket? (Show the children a life jacket.) Life jackets help keep us safe on boats. What else might you do to stay safe on a boat?

➤ How is a sailboat different from a rowboat? A tugboat? A canoe? What is your favorite kind of boat? (Make a list of the boats the children describe.)

WORKING TOGETHER

Invite the children to help you make sailboat salads. Ask the children to wash their hands and then help you clean off a work table surface. Invite the children to arrange lettuce leaves on paper plates. Then place a peach half on each lettuce leaf, flat side up. Show the children how to skewer cheese triangles on pretzel sticks and then stick the pretzel-stick sails into their peach halves. Enjoy eating a super summer salad!

A Banana Boat

MATERIALS

➤ picture of a large bunch of bananas

➤ bananas

➤ a pail of water

➤ peanut butter

➤ butter knives

➤ sunflower seeds

➤ pretzel sticks

➤ square cheese slices (cut in triangular shapes)

➤ paper plates

SHARING TOGETHER

➤ Which fruits do you like to eat in the summer? Do you have a favorite? Which fruit is your favorite? Do you like bananas? Did you know that bananas grow in bunches? (Show the children a picture of a bunch of bananas.) What do you do before you eat a banana? Let's pretend to peel a banana.

➤ Will a banana float or sink in water? Let's try it. Did you guess correctly?

WORKING TOGETHER

Invite the children to make banana boats. Ask the children to wash their hands and then help you clean off a work table surface. Give each child a banana. Help the children peel their bananas, then trim off the outer curved parts to make flat bases. Ask the children to set their bananas on a paper plate, cut-side down. Show the children how to spread peanut butter on the inside curve of their bananas. Invite the children to sprinkle sunflower seeds over the peanut butter. Be aware that some children may have allergies to nuts. Help the children skewer cheese triangles on the pretzel sticks. Stick the pretzel-stick sails into the "banana boats" and enjoy eating smooth sailing snacks!

LEARNING ABOUT PLANTS, ANIMALS, AND INSECTS

SUMMER is a time to explore change and growth in plants, animals, and insects. Through the following activities, children will gain an awareness of the special role seeds play in the life of plants, learn about animals, fish, and birds that are active in the summer, and discover some of the characteristics of insects.

Planting Seeds

MATERIALS

➤ orange and grapefruit seeds

➤ a container of water

➤ soil

➤ small flowerpots

➤ large spoons

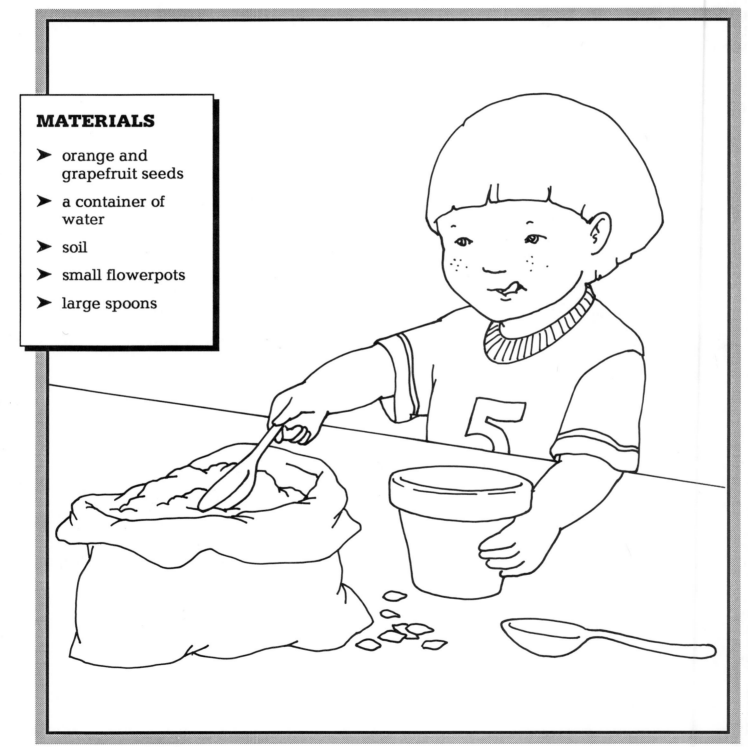

SHARING TOGETHER

➤ Do you know what seeds need to grow? Seeds need air, water, and light. Do you know how to plant a seed? Show me how you would plant a seed. Let's try it together. Do you know how to care for plants? How many of you have plants at home? Do you help your parents take care of the plants? How?

WORKING TOGETHER

Soak orange and grapefruit seeds in water overnight. The next day, invite the children to plant some of the soaked seeds. Help the children use large spoons to fill small flowerpots with soil. Show the children how to plant the soaked orange and grapefruit seeds in the flowerpots. Plant several seeds in each pot and cover the seeds with 1/4" of soil.

Set the flowerpots near a sunny window and water daily. Encourage the children to observe their flowerpots each day. Point out to the children the tiny leaves as they begin to appear. Help the children keep a chart of the plants' growth.

Dip an Apple

MATERIALS

➤ applesauce

➤ apples

➤ small paper cups

➤ a large platter

➤ knife (for adult use only)

➤ paper plates

SHARING TOGETHER

➤ Do apples have seeds? Where are the seeds in an apple? What do you think would happen to apple seeds if you planted them? Do you know how apples grow? Apples grow on trees in apple orchards. Have you ever gone apple-picking? Tell us about it.

➤ What kinds of summer treats can you make from apples? Do you know how to make applesauce? Do you like to eat applesauce? Is applesauce sweet or sour?

WORKING TOGETHER

Ask the children to wash their hands and then help you clean off a work table surface. Slice several apples into eight pieces each. Arrange the apple slices on a large platter. Place the applesauce in paper cups and give a cup to each child. Invite the children to dip apple slices in their applesauce for a doubly-good apple treat.

Popcorn Collage

MATERIALS

➤ poster paper

➤ glue

➤ crayons

➤ popped and unpopped popcorn (save a large bowl of popped popcorn for snacktime)

SHARING TOGETHER

➤ Do you like to eat corn? Did you know that popcorn is corn, too? (Discuss how popcorn is a seed that may be eaten.) Do you like to eat popcorn?

➤ How do you make popcorn? What sound does popcorn make as it is popping? Can you make that sound? Let's pretend to be popcorn popping together.

WORKING TOGETHER

Invite the children to make summer collages out of popcorn. Give each child a piece of poster paper. Encourage the children to arrange and glue popped and unpopped popcorn on their papers in creative designs. Suggest that they use crayons to add details to the popcorn designs as well. When the collages are completely dry, display the children's work on a Sharing Wall in the classroom. Then invite the children to enjoy eating a snack made from seeds—popped popcorn!

An Underwater Scene

MATERIALS

➤ pictures of underwater sea life, including a starfish

➤ crayons

➤ white butcher paper

➤ diluted blue tempera paint

➤ paintbrushes

SHARING TOGETHER

➤ Have you ever gone swimming in the ocean in the summertime? What creatures live in the ocean? Let's name some underwater animals. Have you ever seen a starfish? What do you think a starfish looks like? (Show the children a picture of a starfish.)

➤ What do you think the animals that live in the ocean eat? Did you know that plants live in the ocean, too? (Show the children pictures of underwater sea life, pointing out fish, coral, plants, starfish, and so on. Continue the discussion with the children for as long as they show interest.)

WORKING TOGETHER

Invite the children to make their own underwater summer scenes. Divide the class into small cooperative learning groups. Remind the children to wear paint shirts or smocks. Ask adult volunteers to help the children draw fish, animals, and plants that live in the water on large sheets of butcher paper. Encourage the children to add other details, such as a sandy bottom, pebbles, coral, starfish, jellyfish, seahorses, and so on.

Show the children how to paint over their pictures with diluted blue tempera paint to give their drawings an underwater effect. Encourage the children to describe the variety of plants and animals represented in their underwater pictures. Display the underwater scenes around the classroom. Or use the scenes as a background for a bulletin-board display of the ocean.

A Fish That Swims

MATERIALS

➤ pictures of a variety of fish

➤ plastic foam egg carton cups

➤ permanent marking pens

➤ 8″ squares of nylon netting

➤ rubber bands

➤ a container of water

SHARING TOGETHER

➤ Let's look at pictures of some fish. (Show the children pictures of a variety of fish. Point to the gills.) Do you know what these are? These are called *gills*. Why do you suppose a fish has gills (to breathe)?

➤ What do you think makes a fish a good swimmer (fins, tail)? When you go swimming in the summer, do you kick with your feet to help you swim? Look at the fish's tail. The fish's tail helps the fish swim. How are your feet like a fish's tail?

WORKING TOGETHER

Invite the children to make a fish that swims! Cut egg cartons into individual cups. Invite the children to use permanent marking pens to draw fish eyes, mouths, and gills on the egg carton cups. Help the children cover the egg cups with netting. Secure the netting in place with rubber bands to create fish-shape bodies. Show the children how to place their "fish" in a container of water and then blow on the fish to make them "swim."

Bird Feeder

MATERIALS

➤ pinecones

➤ peanut butter

➤ crushed peanuts, oatmeal, or birdseed

➤ spoons

➤ heavy string

➤ butter knives

SHARING TOGETHER

➤ Do you like to watch the birds in the summer? Tell me what the birds look like. Can you pretend to be a bird? Let's pretend to be a bird flying. What kind of bird are you?

➤ Do you have a bird feeder at home? Have you ever seen a bird feeder? What does a bird feeder look like? Do you know what birds like to eat? Can you pretend to be a bird eating? Let's try together.

WORKING TOGETHER

Invite the children to make their own bird feeders. Give each child a pinecone. Help the children tie heavy string around the tops of the pinecones, leaving enough excess string so the pinecones may be attached to tree branches. Then show the children how to use butter knives to spread peanut butter on their pinecones. Invite the children to spoon crushed peanuts, oatmeal, or birdseed into the peanut butter. Encourage the children to take their pinecone bird feeders home to hang from tree branches. Be sure to make your own bird feeder as well. Hang the bird feeder outside a classroom window so you and the children may enjoy watching the birds feed all year long.

As an alternative to this activity, help the children spread peanut butter on several low branches of a tree near a classroom window. Sprinkle bacon bits or birdseed on the peanut butter. Invite the children to watch as the birds eat from the branches.

Make a Print

MATERIALS

➤ sponges (cut in the shapes of fish and birds)

➤ tempera paint

➤ pie tins

➤ construction paper

➤ crayons

SHARING TOGETHER

➤ Can you pretend to be a fish swimming in the water? Let's try it together. Now let's pretend to be birds flying in the air. How are fish and birds alike? How are fish and birds different? Can fish fly? Can birds swim? I know a bird that can swim. Do you know what bird can swim? Ducks can swim. How are you like a bird? How are you like a fish?

WORKING TOGETHER

Invite the children to make a summer picture of fish and bird prints. Pour different colors of tempera paint in shallow pie tins and place the pie tins on a work table. Give each child a sheet of construction paper. Remind the children to wear paint shirts or smocks. Invite the children to dip fish-shaped and bird-shaped sponges in the tempera paint and then use the sponges to make patterns and designs on the construction paper. After the designs are dry, suggest that the children add details to their prints using crayons. Display the fish and bird prints on a summer Sharing Wall, or encourage the children to take their prints home to share with their families.

Ants on a Log

MATERIALS

➤ peanut butter

➤ raisins

➤ celery stalks

➤ butter knives

SHARING TOGETHER

➤ Have you ever seen ants in the summer? Where? What do you know about ants? Where do ants live? Did you know that ants build anthills? Have you ever watched ants build an anthill? (If possible, take the children outside to observe ants and their anthill.)

WORKING TOGETHER

Before beginning this activity, read a book about ants to the children. Then invite the children to make a fun snack. Ask the children to wash their hands and then help you clean off a work table. Show the children how to use butter knives to spread peanut butter on celery stalks. Then invite the children to arrange raisins on top of the peanut butter to resemble ants on a log. Encourage the children to enjoy eating their "ants on a log" summer snack!

EXPLORING SUMMER THROUGH PLAY AND EXERCISE

CHILDREN have a great opportunity to develop their large motor skills outside during the warm summer months. In this section, children participate in physical activities that promote their sense of balance, increase their motor skill development, and encourage self-confidence in their growing physical abilities.

Walk the Line

MATERIALS

➤ masking tape

➤ cup

➤ water

➤ book

SHARING TOGETHER

➤ Do you like to play hopscotch in the summer? Did you know that balancing is very important in hopscotch? Let's practice balancing. Can you balance on one foot? Let's try it together. Now try balancing on the other foot. Let's try hopping. Hop on your right foot. Now hop on your left foot. Is it hard to keep your balance?

➤ Pretend you are balancing a book on your head. Can you turn around carefully and sit down? You need to be very still and concentrate when you are trying to balance. Do you know what the word *concentrate* means? Concentrate means to think very carefully about what you are doing.

WORKING TOGETHER

Invite the children to practice their balancing skills. Remind the children to concentrate while they are doing this activity. Tape a 10-foot line of masking tape on the floor in an open area of the classroom. Ask the children to walk heel-to-toe along the line, first forward and then backward. Demonstrate for the children how to balance slowly and gracefully, holding their heads up with their arms out at their sides. Once the children have mastered this task, encourage them to walk the line carrying a cup of water. Invite the children to balance a book on their heads, hop, skip, jump, and tiptoe along the line as well.

Follow the Path

MATERIALS

➤ several box lids
or shallow boxes
(wide enough for
children to stand
inside of)

SHARING TOGETHER

➤ Can you pretend to tiptoe by a sleeping kitten? Let's try it together. Now follow me around the classroom. Can you move as I do? Let's see. (Play a modified version of follow-the-leader, making simple movements, such as walking with arms outstretched, hands on your head, skipping, and so on.)

➤ Do you like to go on hikes in the summer? Where have you gone? Did you follow a path? What did you see on your hike?

WORKING TOGETHER

Invite the children to make a special path to follow in the classroom. Ask the children to help you place box lids or shallow boxes along the classroom floor to make a path. Encourage the children to take turns following the path, stepping carefully into and out of each lid or box, one foot at a time. Remind the children to concentrate, moving carefully as they follow the path. Then invite the children to make a variety of other paths for more practice.

Knock Them Over

MATERIALS

➤ a model or picture of a triangle

➤ 10 soft drink cans

➤ medium-size ball

SHARING TOGETHER

➤ Can you catch a beach ball? Throw a baseball? Dribble a basketball? Let's pretend to catch a ball together. What other ball games do you play in the summer?

➤ Have you ever gone bowling? Tell us about it. What kind of ball do you use when you go bowling? Do you know what to do with a bowling ball?

WORKING TOGETHER

Invite the children to bowl using a ball and several soft-drink cans. First, show the children what a triangle looks like. Then ask the children to help you arrange ten soft-drink cans on the floor in the shape of a triangle. The front row should have one can and the last row should have four. Draw a line a short distance from the cans. Encourage the children to take turns rolling or throwing a ball from the line toward the cans to knock over as many cans as possible. Ask a child who has already had a turn to help you reset the cans for the next child.

Hot Potato Game

MATERIALS

➤ large potato

➤ music (optional)

SHARING TOGETHER

➤ Raise your hand if you like to play catch outside in the summer. When you play catch, do you sometimes drop the ball? What happens when you drop the ball? You try again, right? Who do you play catch with in your family? Let's pretend we are playing catch together. (Gather the children together in a circle and pretend to throw the ball to each child. Encourage the children to pretend to catch and throw the ball.)

WORKING TOGETHER

Invite the children to play "Hot Potato." Ask the children to sit together with you in a circle on the floor in a large, carpeted area of the classroom. Have the children pass a potato around the circle. Explain to the children that when you say "hot potato," the child who is left holding the potato may leave the circle. Continue the game until all the players have left the circle. Or, you may use music for the game, if desired. Play the music, and when the music stops, the child left holding the "hot potato" leaves the circle.

Bat a Balloon

MATERIALS

➤ small paper plates

➤ crayons or marking pens

➤ tongue depressors

➤ superglue or heavy-duty stapler

➤ balloons

SHARING TOGETHER

➤ Do you like balloons? Watch while I blow up this balloon. What happens if I blow the balloon up too much? Let's pretend to blow up balloons. How big is your balloon?

➤ What games do you play in the summer with a ball? Do you play tag with a ball? How about baseball? How about catch? How is a balloon like a ball?

WORKING TOGETHER

Invite the children to play a game using a balloon. Gather the children around a large work table. Give each child a small paper plate and a tongue depressor. Help the children print their names on their plates and then invite the children to decorate the paper plates with a summer design. Suggest that children decorate both sides of the plates as well as the tongue depressors. Glue or staple the tongue depressors to the decorated plates for a handle.

Blow up several balloons and tie the ends. Show the children how to use their decorated plates to bat a balloon into the air. Once the children have mastered this task, divide the class into pairs and encourage the children to bat the balloons back and forth between them. Remind the children that it is okay if they miss the balloon because it takes practice to be able to do this activity well. Invite the children to take their bats and balloons home to play with as well.

ENJOYING SPECIAL SUMMER DAYS

CHILDREN learn about their heritage and the heritage of others by celebrating special holidays with family and friends. During the holiday activities provided here, the children participate in exploring customs associated with Father's Day and the Fourth of July, as well as making holiday gifts and decorations.

A Storage Box for Dad, Stepdad, or Grandpa

MATERIALS

➤ shoeboxes

➤ glue

➤ material scraps

➤ marking pens or crayons

SHARING TOGETHER

➤ What does your dad, stepdad, or grandpa like to do? Does he like to read? Does he like to play games? What games do you like to play with your dad, stepdad, or grandpa?

➤ How do you help your dad, stepdad, or grandpa? Do you help him do chores around the house? What chores do you help him with? How does your dad, stepdad, or grandpa help you? Does he help you play games? Does he help you with your chores? What chores does he help you with?

WORKING TOGETHER

Explain to the children that Father's Day is a special summer holiday. Invite the children to make gifts for their dads, stepdads, or grandpas for Father's Day. Give each child a shoebox. Help the children decorate the shoeboxes by gluing scraps of material on every side. When the glue has dried, encourage the children to use marking pens or crayons to add details to their boxes. Suggest to the children that they give the boxes to their dads, stepdads, or grandpas on Father's Day to use as storage or keepsake boxes.

A Litter Bag for Dad, Stepdad, or Grandpa

MATERIALS

➤ medium-size brown paper bags

➤ marking pens or crayons

➤ yarn or pipe cleaners

➤ hole punch

SHARING TOGETHER

➤ Do you like to ride in the car? Where do you go when you ride in the car? Do you ever have snacks in the car? Where do you put the litter? Do you know what a litter bag is?

WORKING TOGETHER

Invite the children to make litter bags for their dads, stepdads, or grandpas for Father's Day. Give each child a brown paper bag. Encourage the children to use marking pens or crayons to decorate the bags with colorful designs. Then help the children fold down the tops of the bags and punch two holes along the folded edge. Thread the yarn or pipe cleaners through the holes and tie to form hanging loops. Encourage the children to give the litter bags to their dads, stepdads, or grandpas on Father's Day to hang in the family car.

A Patriotic Headband

MATERIALS

➤ cardboard strips (one per child)

➤ marking pens or crayons

➤ staplers

➤ gummed stars

➤ glitter

➤ glue

SHARING TOGETHER

➤ Did you know that the 4th of July is America's birthday? How do you celebrate the 4th of July? Have you ever seen fireworks? What do fireworks look like? What do fireworks sound like? Let's pretend to be 4th of July fireworks together.

➤ Have you ever been to a 4th of July parade? What things do you see in a 4th of July parade? Do you see flags? How about clowns? What other things do you see in a 4th of July parade?

WORKING TOGETHER

Invite the children to make headbands to wear during a celebration for the 4th of July. Give each child a cardboard strip. Encourage the children to use marking pens or crayons, gummed stars, and glitter to decorate their strips. Then fit the decorated strips around the children's heads and carefully staple the ends of the strips together to make headbands. Encourage the children to wear their patriotic headbands in a 4th of July parade around the classroom and then wear the headbands home to share with their families.

A Patriotic Poster

MATERIALS

➤ an American flag

➤ red and blue marking pens or crayons

➤ gummed stars (white or silver)

➤ white sheets of construction paper

➤ 18" dowel sticks (one per child)

➤ tape

SHARING TOGETHER

➤ Let's look at an American flag together. What colors are on the American flag? Do you put a flag up at home on the 4th of July?

➤ What shapes do you see on the American flag? Do you see circles? Do you know why there are 50 stars on the American flag? Because there are 50 states in America. There is a star on the flag for each state in America. Do you know what state we live in?

WORKING TOGETHER

Invite the children to make their own American flags. Show the children an American flag. Point out the shapes and colors of the flag. Discuss the significance of the stars on the flag as well.

Give each child a sheet of white construction paper. Help the children use marking pens or crayons and gummed stars to decorate the construction paper like the American flag. Encourage the children to tape their flags to dowel sticks and wave the flags in a summer 4th of July marching parade around the classroom.

EXPLORING SUMMER THROUGH ART

ART ACTIVITIES provide a fun, productive way of learning all about summer. Using different materials, the children can make splatter paintings, shell pails, and even a smiling summer T-shirt!

Summer Stones

MATERIALS

➤ rocks

➤ tempera paint

➤ small paintbrushes or Q-tips

➤ glue

➤ felt scraps

SHARING TOGETHER

➤ What do you like to do in the summer? Do you like to play games? What games do you like to play? Do you like to look at the flowers? What kinds of flowers do you like? What kinds of animals do you see in the summer?

➤ What things remind you of summer? Do snowballs remind you of summer? How about beach balls? What other things do you see outside that remind you of summer?

WORKING TOGETHER

Invite the children to make special summer paperweights. Give each child a rock or have the children choose the rocks they would like to work with. Remind the children to wear paint shirts or smocks. Invite the children to paint their rocks to represent things that remind them of summer, such as a face, an animal, a beach ball, flower, tree, and so on. Show the children how to use paintbrushes and Q-tips to make their pictures on the rocks. When the rock paintings are dry, help the children glue pieces of felt to the rock bottoms. Then encourage the children to take their rocks home to use as paperweights.

Splatter Painting

MATERIALS

➤ toothbrushes

➤ a screen mounted on a wooden frame

➤ large sheets of construction paper

➤ cardboard shapes (circles, squares, rectangles, and triangles)

➤ tempera paints

SHARING TOGETHER

➤ Show several different shapes to the children. Discuss what each shape is called (square, triangle, and so on.) Can you find something outside that is shaped like a square? Let's look. Can you find something outside that is shaped like a circle? What do you see in the classroom that is shaped like a circle? (Continue this discussion with a variety of different shapes.)

WORKING TOGETHER

Give each child a large sheet of construction paper. Remind the children to wear paint shirts or smocks. Invite the children to arrange cardboard shapes on the sheets of construction paper to make pictures of boats or other summer scenes. Then have the children take turns placing a screen, mounted on a wooden frame, over their pictures. Using toothbrushes dipped in tempera paint, help each child "scrub" over the screen. Remind the children not to put the toothbrushes in their mouths. Remove the screen and cardboard pieces carefully to reveal summer splatter pictures. Display the paintings on a Sharing Wall in the classroom.

A Shell Pail

MATERIALS

➤ nut cans with plastic lids

➤ blue fabric

➤ glue

➤ paintbrushes

➤ thick yarn

➤ variety of shells

➤ pieces of coral

SHARING TOGETHER

➤ Have you ever walked along a beach in the summertime? What did you see on the beach? Snow? Sand? Do you like to play in the sand? What kinds of things can you do in the sand?

➤ Have you ever seen a seashell? What did it look like? Let's look at some seashells together. Can you see different colors in the shells? What colors do you see?

WORKING TOGETHER

Invite the children to examine a variety of seashells. Discuss the different kinds and colors. Then encourage the children to make their own shell pails. Give each child a nut can with a plastic lid. (Before beginning this activity, drill a hole in the sides of each of the cans.) Then help the children cut pieces of fabric to fit around the sides of the cans and glue the fabric in place. Cut pieces of yarn long enough to make handles for the pails. Show the children how to insert the yarn ends into the holes on the sides of the cans. Make a knot at the end of each yarn piece on the inside of the cans. Help the children use paintbrushes to spread glue around the lower edges of the cloth-covered cans. Invite the children to glue on shells, such as starfish, seahorses, and any other kinds of shells that would be appropriate for the sizes of the cans. Add bits and pieces of coral as well.

After the glue has dried, invite the children to fill their cans with the remaining shells. With the help of adult or student volunteers, take the children to a beach, if one is nearby. Be sure to obtain signed field-trip permission slips from the children's parents.

Sand Painting

MATERIALS

➤ sand (dark and light)

➤ cardboard

➤ all-purpose white glue

➤ small paintbrushes

➤ pencils

➤ water

SHARING TOGETHER

➤ Have you ever walked on a beach? How does it feel to walk in the sand? Does it feel soft? How does it feel to play in the sand?

➤ Let's look carefully at some sand. Do you see all the different colors? There are different colors in the sand because sand is made of tiny rocks that have been ground into tiny pieces by the ocean. What colors do you see in the sand? Do you see a red piece of sand? What other colors do you see?

WORKING TOGETHER

Invite the children to make sand paintings. Give each child a piece of cardboard. Encourage the children to draw simple summer designs with a pencil. Suggest that they draw one object on the cardboard, such as a boat, sun with rays, or a fish. Help the children decide how and where in the designs to use the two colors of sand.

Mix glue with an equal amount of water. Invite the children to paint one small area of their drawings with the glue mixture and then sprinkle the sand over it. Show the children how to shake off the extra sand and paint glue on the next portion. Continue until all the parts of their pictures using the first selected color of sand are done. When the glue begins to dry, fill in the remaining portion of the designs with the other color of sand. Display the sand paintings on a Sharing Wall in the classroom when they are completely dry.

Summer Can Be Silly

MATERIALS

➤ magazines

➤ construction paper

➤ white sheets of paper

➤ round-edged scissors

➤ glue

SHARING TOGETHER

➤ Are you ever silly? Do you think a clown is silly? Who is the silliest person that you know? Let's all be silly together. When I say "go," everyone be silly. When I say "stop," everyone be still. Ready?

WORKING TOGETHER

Gather the children around a large work table or divide the class into smaller cooperative working groups. Set the materials listed on page 72 on the table within easy reach of the children. Give each child a pair of round-edged scissors and a sheet of white paper. Invite the children to make the silliest pictures they can think of using the materials on the table, such as a baby's face with a dog's body, a person walking on water, and so on. Help the children cut out the pictures from magazines or cut shapes from construction paper. Encourage the children to look over all the pictures and decide which of the pictures is the silliest! Display the finished pictures on a bulletin board labeled "It's a Silly Summer!"

A Smiling Summer T-Shirt

MATERIALS

➤ cotton T-shirts (brought from home)

➤ iron-on crayons (you can find them at a hobby or craft shop)

➤ paper

➤ pencils

➤ straight pins

➤ ironing board

➤ iron

SHARING TOGETHER

➤ What is the weather like in the summer where you live? Is it cold in the summer? Is it hot in the summer? Does it rain? What do you like to wear in the summer? Do you wear mittens? What do you wear when you go out to play?

WORKING TOGETHER

Invite the children to make special summer T-shirts. Each child will need to bring from home a clean, solid-colored cotton T-shirt, preferably white. Have the children use pencils to draw a simple smiling object on a scrap piece of paper, such as a child's face, the sun, a sunflower, a star, and so on. Using the iron-on crayons, help the children copy the designs they made on a clean sheet of paper by pressing down heavily with the iron-on crayons to get a strong color. Then pin the children's designs, face down, on T-shirts. Run a heated iron back and forth over the designs, pressing down firmly. Be sure to use the hot iron out of reach of the children. Lift up a corner of the paper to see if the design has transferred.

When finished, be sure to remove all the pins from the T-shirts and place the iron and ironing board out of the reach of the children. After the designs are set on each T-shirt, invite the children to try on their new smiling summer T-shirts over their clothes and wear them home!

Oh! What an Octopus!

MATERIALS

➤ picture of an octopus

➤ paper bag

➤ old newspaper

➤ construction paper

➤ paste or tape

➤ marking pens or crayons

➤ round-edged scissors

SHARING TOGETHER

➤ Where do octopuses live? What does an octopus look like? (Show the children a picture of an octopus.) How many arms does an octopus have? Let's count the octopus' arms together. What would you do if you had eight arms like an octopus? Do you think it would be fun to be an octopus? Can you pretend to be an octopus? Let's try together.

WORKING TOGETHER

Invite the children to make an octopus out of paper! Give each child a paper bag. Ask the children to tear newspaper into small pieces. Then have children wad up the newspaper pieces and pack them into their bags until the bags are as large as they want their octopuses to be. Help the children fold the tops of the bags over and paste or tape the tops down.

Show the children how to cut eight narrow, long strips of construction paper to serve as arms. Help the children paste the strips to the folded ends of the paper bags. After the paste is dry, curl the ends of the strips by rolling them around a pencil several times. Invite the children to make faces on their octopuses with marking pens or crayons. Display the octopuses in the classroom, or encourage the children to take their octopuses home to share with their families.

Bibliography of Children's Books

Reading good books to children opens up worlds of information and stimulates imaginations! Establish an early love of reading in children by creating positive experiences with these seasonal selections. Use one or more of these books to introduce an activity, as a follow-up to an activity, or for individual use by the children during independent time.

BOOKS TO ENJOY DURING THE SUMMER

Barn Dance, Bill Martin, Jr., and John Archambault, Holt, 1986.

A Beach Day, Douglas Florian, Greenwillow Books, 1990.

Better Not Get Wet, Jesse Bear, Nancy White Carlstrom, Macmillan, 1988.

Big Red Barn, Margaret Wise Brown, Harper & Row, 1989.

It Looked Like Spilt Milk, Charles G. Shaw, Harper & Row, 1947.

Jennie's Hat, Ezra Jack Keats, Harper & Row, 1966.

The Lady and the Spider, Faith McNulty, Harper & Row, 1986.

Mr. Gumpy's Outing, John Burningham, Holt, 1970.

The Napping House, Audrey Wood, Harcourt Brace Jovanovich, 1984.

Once We Went on a Picnic, Aileen Fisher, Crowell, 1975.

Over the Meadow, Ezra Jack Keats, Four Winds Press, 1971.

The Popcorn Book, Tomie de Paola, Holiday House, 1978.

Rain Makes Applesauce, Julian Scheer, Holiday House, 1964.

The Reason for a Flower, Ruth Heller, Grosset & Dunlap, 1983.

The Relatives Came, Cynthia Rylant, Bradbury Press, 1985.

The Rose in My Garden, Anita Lobel, Greenwillow Books, 1984.

The Very Busy Spider, Eric Carle, Philomel Books, 1984.

OTHER BOOKS TO ENJOY THROUGHOUT THE YEAR

Annie and the Wild Animals, Jan Brett, Houghton Mifflin, 1985.

Calico Cat's Year, Donald Charles, Childrens Press, 1984.

First Comes Spring, Anne Rockwell, Crowell, 1985.

Frederick, Leo Lionni, Pantheon, 1967.

Growing Vegetable Soup, Lois Ehlert, Harcourt Brace Jovanovich, 1987.

Haircuts for the Woolseys, Tomie de Paola, Putnam Publishing Group, 1989.

The Little House, Virginia Lee Burton, Houghton Mifflin, 1942.

New Boots for Spring, Harriet Ziefert and Deborah Kogan Ray, Viking Press, 1989.

Ox-Cart Man, Donald Hall, Puffin Books, 1979.

Sunshine Makes the Seasons, Franklyn M. Branley, Crowell, 1974.

A Year in the Country, Douglas Florian, Greenwillow Books, 1989.